The rattycorner.co

Rat Care Guide

Annette Rand

CONTENTS

INTRODUCTION

These pages contain my own opinions on the best way to keep rats. I have owned rats since 2001 and have been breeding them since 2008, so I aim to provide the information you need to make your own choices. I own an extensive collection of books about rat keeping, and find many of them contradictory or just plain out of date. Standards of husbandry and ethics have moved on over the years, but all I can give you is my own experience, feelings and opinions.

Rats are becoming an extremely popular pet, being easy to keep in a relatively small space and very engaging and friendly if raised and handled properly. Rats are not as low maintenance as many other rodents - they benefit from daily interaction with their humans and their cages need frequent attention, with a tidy up each day or two and a full clean out each week or so. I'd put their smell/cage cleaning factor at about hamster level - they need cleaning more often than gerbils, less often than mice.

Because they are so sociable, it's unfair to keep a rat on its own. They need to have the company of their own kind because it's impossible for you to be with them all the time. Rats can usually be kept in single sex groups without problems, thus giving the perfect excuse for getting more than one!

Wild rats are crepuscular, which is a word I really love. It means they are mostly awake during the hours of dawn and dusk. To be honest, rats are so adaptable and opportunistic that they're only crepuscular when it suits them. Your pets will easily adapt themselves to your routine, and will soon come to know when it's time to expect food and when it's to come out and play.

Some people find that they have allergy problems with rats, so it may be as well to handle someone else's rats before spending a lot of money setting up a rat cage. Adult males are possibly more allergenic than females, although neutering can help. Do also bear in mind that it's also fairly common to become allergic to a particular cage substrate rather than the rats themselves.

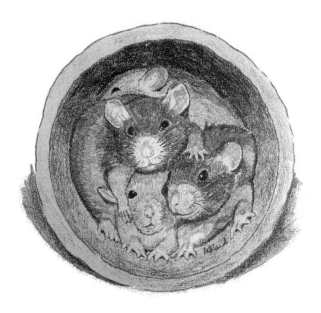

SOURCING YOUR RATS

Rescue rats

A rescue is an organisation or an individual that has taken in the rats with the aim of rehoming them. You may be required to undergo a home check before adopting rescue rats. I don't see this as a disadvantage because it shows that the rescuer is concerned about their wellbeing, although it can then restrict you to homing rats from rescues which cover your home area.

Rescue adults vary from the well socialised to the traumatised and aggressive. You may find yourself paying out a lot in vet fees and spending a lot of your time on an older rescue, but often this is the time when you bond most closely. It's a gamble but very rewarding to take on adult rescue rats.

Rescue kittens are generally those born to adults taken into rescue. Giving a home to young rats is less of a gamble than homing an older rat, especially if the rescue or foster home has spent time socialising the youngsters. You will most likely receive little or no information on their hereditary disease resistance or tendency to develop tumours.

Breeder rats

There are many people who breed rats for many different reasons. What you need to be looking for is the 'reputable breeder'. This is complicated by the fact that there are as many definitions of a reputable breeder as there are people looking to find one, so what you really need to look for is someone whose ethics and viewpoint coincide with your own.

I would like to emphasise one point. Don't be reluctant to approach a breeder just because you are not intending to show your rats. Every breeder has kittens to home on occasion, and there is no reason to suppose that you wouldn't provide the kind of home they are looking for.

You will probably have to go on a waiting list for a breeder rat, especially if you are seeking a particular variety. If you ask to be added to the waiting list of several breeders, it is courteous to let them know if you have found your rats elsewhere, so please keep a record of who you have applied to.

One good reason for turning to a breeder is to find rats with good health and temperament. These are factors which can be bred for, so you are looking for someone who keeps good records of their lines and who uses these to influence their breeding decisions. These breeders will be keen to keep in touch with the new owners of their kittens. Ask about health and temperament.

You may also want to ask the breeder about their breeding practices and ethics:

Do they use a questionnaire to find out about prospective owners? You should be prepared to be given a questionnaire or be 'interviewed' for you suitability to take on your new pets. This shows that the breeder cares what happens to the lives they have brought into the world. Some breeders prefer to have an informal chat, others (like myself) prefer to take written details at first.

Will you be asked to sign a contract? Many breeders will ask you to sign a contract, with restrictions on the breeding and rehoming of their rats and preferences for their welfare. Others will not, feeling that the contract is unenforceable, but will still have expectations as to the care of the rats.

Will you be asked to keep in touch? Regular updates help the breeder to monitor the health and wellbeing of their lines. You should expect to be asked to give regular updates.

Do they home their rats in same sex pairs or groups only? Rats are very social creatures. They need interaction with others of their own kind and preferably of a similar age. It is common for breeders to refuse to home single rats because of this.

Can you visit the rattery? This allows you to see the conditions in which the rats are kept at home, possibly meet the parents. It's a nice idea, but not always feasible given that some breeders are also working full time, have other commitments, may have rats susceptible to infection from visitors, or have had bad experiences in the past with bringing people into their home.

Do they do a home visit? Again this isn't always possible, though it would be an ideal.

Do they cull their litters? Does your breeder cull their litters down to make them a more manageable size for their does? Does this make a difference to your feeling comfortable with taking kittens from them and feeling comfortable with them as a person?

Do they cull or rehome their retirees? It's a question to ask, although I don't know anyone who admits to culling their ex-breeders.

Do they take back any rats that can no longer be kept by their new owners? This offer is another indication that the breeder is prepared to accept responsibility for the lives they have brought into the world.

Do they provide holiday rat sitting? As above, although this can be limited by space and other circumstances.

Pet shop rats

Buying from a pet shop tends to make the whole process very quick and easy, which, although it sounds good, isn't always the best thing. These are living creatures that you are taking on responsibility for, and you need to take time to consider this and to plan for their care.

Some pet shops do not guarantee the sex of the pets they sell. Many of the accidental litters offered for homing on rat forums and mailing lists are the result of pet shops mis-sexing their rats, or separating the male and female babies too late. The in joke is that you 'buy one, get twelve free'.

Pet shop rats are often separated from their mother too early, looking undersized and still in their baby fur when offered for sale.

Poor advice is often given on the size and type of cage required. To give the pets shops the benefit of the doubt, I'm guessing this is because they usually see tiny young rats and don't realise that they can grow into a relatively large adult.

The rats have no history given, often only an approximate age, and no information is fed back to the breeder. The only way that a breeder can select for good health and temperament is by gathering information through contact throughout the life of the pet. There is no facility for this from a pet shop rat.

The rats may originate from pet stock or a feeder/pet supplier farm, with overbred females and lack of selection for health. Farmed rats are not handled frequently enough during the crucial early period when young rats bond with humans.

The rats are sometimes not handled enough while in the shop, leaving the new owner with nervous or aggressive pets.

Because of these points, I believe that live animals should not be sold in shops, and would not support the shops by buying from them. Buying a rat from a pet shop helps the individual rat, but encourages the shop to restock, which in turn encourages the breeding of more stock. I'm not going to condemn anyone who does buy from pet shops, though, as I completely understand the urge to take the individual rat out of there.

Rehoming older rats

It's quite common for older rats to be offered for rehoming, usually because their owner's circumstances have changed and they no longer have time for them. There are some very sweet rats to be found this way, but also some unhandled nightmares.

CHOOSING YOUR RATS

Which sex?

Females (Does)

Females are generally more agile and active than males, although you'll find that the rats haven't always been told this. They remain smaller than the males and have softer fur. Their major health problem is with mammary tumours, although if you source your rats from a reputable breeder you will be able to ask them about the incidence of mammary lumps in their lines. These tumours can be operated on and removed fairly easily, and contrary to what some people will tell you, they don't always come back straight away. Adult females will generally weigh between 300 and 550 grams, depending on their breeding and past nutrition.

Males (Bucks)

Male rats are slower and more laid back than females, but this is just the general rule and there are many exceptions. Male rats also tend to scent mark, which means they often leave a small drop of urine on you just to say that you belong to them. Adult males will weigh between 400 and 800 grams, depending on their breeding and past nutrition.

Sexing

Male rats have very obvious testicles by the time they're old enough to go to a new home. If you can't be sure which sex a rat is, it's probably female. It's always best to check for yourself when taking on new rats – don't take someone's word for it.

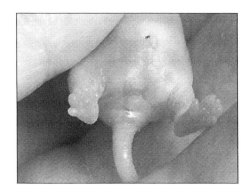

Female at four days old

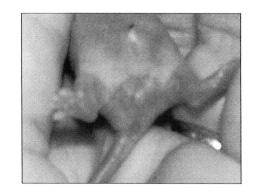

Male at four days old

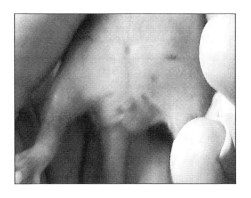

Female at eleven days old

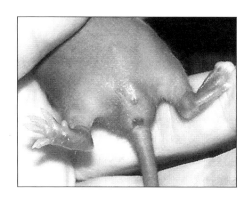

Male at ten days old

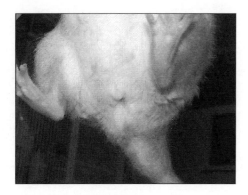
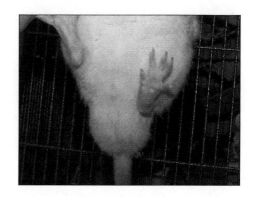

Adult female   *Adult male*

Collecting your rats

If you're collecting rats from a breeder you may not be able to choose which of the babies you have, but if you do, begin by offering your hand to the rats to see which ones choose you. If at a pet shop, ask if you can hold the rats to see how well socialised they are. For a first time owner I would avoid choosing any rat that shows obvious signs of aggression or is very nervous. Check that their eyes are bright and clear, their fur is in good condition, and hold them against your ear to check for signs of respiratory disease. Do not feel obliged to take a rat you are not happy with. It's better to upset someone than to take on a sick or aggressive rat that you weren't planning on.

When you bring your new rats home you may find that their poo is very loose and smelly at first, either all the time or when you take them out of the cage. This is a stress reaction and will settle down once they feel more at home. Young rats who have been on a high protein diet may also have a stronger than usual smell for a while.

HABITAT

Cage or something different?

While an aquarium can provide a safe environment for a rat with a young litter, cages are always the better option in my opinion. They provide better ventilation, slowing the build-up of ammonia in the bedding which can damage your rats' lungs, they let you hang toys and ropes across the cage more easily, and also allow your rats to fulfil their natural inclination to climb.

Some owners find that using a hutch provides a cosy home for their rats. These benefit from being modified to allow the attachment of toys and climbing opportunities.

Choosing a cage

Cage choice seems to be a very individual thing, but there are certain points you need to bear in mind.

Your rats' cage needs to be big enough to allow them to express their natural behaviour. The minimum I would recommend for a pair of rats is 80cm x 50cm x 50cm, as they not only need space to live and play, but also space for cage furniture. Within reason, the bigger the better, although nervous rats may benefit from a smaller space to begin with, while they get used to interacting with you.

Another consideration is ease of access. If your rats are a little timid, you need to be able to reach them. If the cage is difficult to clean out, you're not going to want to do it. Look for a cage with a nice big door positioned to allow you access to all corners of the cage and which will be easy to hang hammocks and ropes across. If you like to tip out the substrate straight into the bin, look for a base which will fit easily through any doors.

My personal preferred cage is the Liberta Explorer, a tall cage which is 90cm wide, 60cm deep and 120cm high, set upon a stand and with large doors that open to the full width of the cage. I use this as an open space without a level halfway down, but with hammocks and ropes to break any falls, and I use custom made metal shelves in the base to replace the shallow plastic trays which come as standard. There is also a similar but more solid (and expensive) cage called the Savic Royal Suite.

Cage position

Well socialised rats will also be eager for your company and will enjoy living in an area you spend a lot of time in. It's best to keep them out of draughts, and also away from strong sunlight as this runs the risk of letting them overheat, and they are not an animal that enjoys a lot of sun. I also prefer to position the cage off the floor where it's easier to interact with the rats. Remember to keep the cage away from any curtains and upholstery that you'd prefer to remain intact, and out of reach of young children.

Litter trays

Most rats will learn to use a litter tray in my experience, especially if trays are placed in the back corners of the cage.

Substrate

There is a lot of debate as to whether wood shavings are a suitable litter for rats. Certainly sawdust and any other dusty substrate can cause sneezing. I would recommend a chopped cardboard substrate, but other substrates include hemp, 100% paper based cat litter (not clumping litter) and, depending on viewpoint, non-perfumed dust extracted wood shavings with large curls of wood. Do consider the feel of the litter for the rats to walk on. Walking on some brands of cat litter looks like walking barefoot across a pebble beach.

Bedding

If you use shredded paper for bedding, please check that the edges are not sharp. I've seen some rats with nasty cuts to their feet from shredded paper.

My preference is for hanging up cheap toilet rolls in the cage, either threaded on ropes or on parrot toys. This not only gives them a soft bedding but also a lot of entertainment bedecking the cage with paper. Another fun option is to put their bedding on the outside of the cage, but positioned so that they can pull it in. A much better solution than letting them pull the curtains or your clothes in through the bars!

Cage furnishings

A range of activities and furnishings for the cage helps to keep rats fit and entertained. They're intelligent animals and can become stir crazy without any stimulation, and are also much more entertaining if they have something to do.

Boxes

Boxes are the perfect rat toy; easy to obtain, usually free, fun to modify for both you and your rats, and disposable when they become too 'ratty'. Just pop an empty box into the cage, or spend some time making a rat castle out of a collection of boxes.

Use smaller boxes to hide treats or even their daily food in. Empty toilet rolls can be folded down at each end to hide treats inside.

Tunnels

The perfect place to sit and eat, or lie and doze. You can save large packing tubes for them, scrounge plastic pipe from road workers, make your own from papier mache around an old pop bottle, or even spend some money and buy them. They can sit in the base of the cage, attach to the sides, or thread onto ropes strung across the cage.

Hammocks

Rats love a hammock or two to lounge in. There are a wide variety available commercially, but they are also very easy to make, at their simplest being a tea towel with a paperclip in each corner.

Ropes

Ropes are fun to balance across and climb up. You can make your own from plaited strips of (unwanted) bed sheets, or purchase them as parrot toys. Thread curtain rings on them to hang other toys from.

Ledges and perches

These are often sold for parrots or chinchillas, but will be appreciated by your rats.

Swings

Most rats are surprisingly quick to get used to moving perches or swinging hammocks.

Plastic huts

Plastic igloos and shelters are commonly sold for small animals, and will be appreciated as a place to sleep when the temperature is lower, or when your rats get older and less able to climb.

Toilet rolls, wrapping paper and tissue paper

Rats love paper. Toilet rolls are fun toys to hang in the cage, starting the roll for them so they can pull it down. Wrapping paper and tissue paper is fun either inside the cage, or within reach outside so the rats have to pull it in through the bars. They will also enjoy pulling in pages of old phone books hung on the outside of the cage.

Wheels

Some rats love their wheel, others will completely ignore it. If you decide to get a wheel, look for one that is at least 28cm across to avoid putting strain on your rat's back, and for a solid wheel with no risk of trapping tails.

Make sure wheel is strong enough to support the weight of the rat; there are some wheels which are just too flexible on their spindle to support an adult rat. The makes I would recommend are the Wodent Wheel and the Silent Spinner.

Prolonged use of the wheel can bring on 'wheel tail', which is a curving of the tail over the back. This seems to be a habit rather than any physical disorder, as the rats are perfectly capable of straightening their tail when they need to balance. My feeling is that the benefits of the exercise outweigh the effect on the look of your rat, and that the wheel-running rat would suffer from being deprived of their wheel.

BEHAVIOUR

Alpha

Most groups of rats will have one 'alpha' who is the most dominant. A rat may remain alpha into old age purely by force of habit, and cages can erupt into dominance fighting after the death of an old alpha. This usually calms down once a new boss rat takes their place. If you find a particular rat is being bullied to the point where it is affecting their wellbeing, you may need to either split the group or have the bully neutered and let the group establish a new pecking order. This can lead to a cascade of neutering.

Biting

Rats rarely bite, and when they do they usually have a reason. This can be simply due to mistaking your hand for food, from fear if the rat has not been socialised well, or from hormonal aggression which if extreme can be solved by castration or spaying.

Many perfectly amenable rats will instinctively bite a finger put through the cage bars. It's a good idea never to offer food through the bars, as this will encourage this behaviour. Both adults and children seem to have an unthinking impulse to poke their fingers into cages, so it's wise to warn them in advance.

Head tilt and rolling

Tilting the head, circling and rolling are all signs of an inner ear infection. See the health care section.

Head weaving

Some rats, particularly those with paler eyes, will tend to weave their head from side to side. This is a way of coping with particularly poor eyesight, helping them to judge distance better.

Mounting

Both males and females will mount rats of the same sex. Males use this as a form of dominance, whereas females will tend to chase and mount cage-mates who are in season.

Socialising

Rats from a reputable breeder should have been handled and socialised from an early age. If you have an unhandleable or biting rat, you will need to take time for them to learn to trust you. A jumpy rat can learn very quickly if you spend a lot of time together. Try wearing two layers of clothes and popping the rat between the layers while you go about your normal routine. Treats of a food such as pieces of puffed rice cereal can help too. If the rat bites when taking food, try putting a little yoghurt on a teaspoon. The jarring of biting down on a spoon soon teaches the rat to take care, and the nature of the food stops them running away with it.

Seasons

Female rats come into season every four or five days. Some rats show strong signs of being in season such as squeakiness, fluttering their ears and arching their bodies (called lordosis), others give very little outward sign. Frequent biting and aggression during seasons, or being stuck in season, can be a sign of polycystic ovaries and is usually helped by spaying.

Bruxing and boggling

Boggling is a very strange rat habit. When a rat is happy it will grind its teeth together, called bruxing. Because the jawbone and its muscle are so close to the eye, extreme bruxing can turn into boggling, which is popping in and out of the eyes. It's harmless and very entertaining. Rats also brux when extremely **un**happy, in the same way that cats sometimes purr when unhappy, presumably in an effort to soothe themselves.

Bog brushing

An amusing term for the habit of fluffing the fur up when riled, often accompanied by scent marking from the flank glands and making a foofing sound. Bog brushing is a sign of aggression or hormonal upset. Be very careful when approaching a bog brushed rat; they may bite before they realise it's you.

Chewing

Rats chew. It's what 'rodent' means. It's a good idea to have a set of clothes that you're not too fond of to wear with the rats. They will chew your clothes, your curtains, your chairs and even wallpaper and carpets. Block things off, hide things, or live with it.

Although your rat will appreciate wooden chew toys, they're not essential. They can keep their teeth perfectly well trimmed by bruxing and normal chewing.

INTRODUCING NEW RATS

Sooner or later, if you're going to follow the advice of not keeping single rats, you'll end up wanting to introduce new friends to your rats. The difficult part here is that rats are such little individuals that every intro goes differently, but there are a number of tips and tricks you can use to help the process along.

Bear in mind that sometimes it just doesn't work, so if you're bringing in new rats you need to have a plan B in case you find yourself with two groups.

Kitten to kitten

Combining two groups of kittens under 13 weeks or so is generally just a case of popping them into a cleaned out cage and letting them make friends.

Adult buck to kitten buck

Most adult bucks will accept young kittens under 9 or 10 weeks or so really easily using the bare cage intro (below). There's a fairly narrow window of time where the kittens are old enough and robust enough to introduced, but young enough not to smell like a challenge to the older rats. It helps to add two or more kittens at once so that they have an ally and playmate.

There is, of course, potential for the youngsters to be hurt or killed if things go wrong, so you do need to take care. Some adult bucks just don't want kittens added to their group, but mostly they will flip and smell the babies and carry on. Problems sometimes arise when the kittens don't know when to stop, and continue to bug their elders even when they've been warned off.

Adult doe to kitten doe

Some does can be reluctant to accept new kittens into the cage, and if initial intros don't go too well, just waiting until the kittens are a little older and able to stick up for themselves can make a big difference. Again, I would recommend bringing in two or more kittens so they have a playmate of a similar age.

Adult buck to adult buck

This is generally the most difficult intro to do successfully, but sometimes you're lucky and it just works. Neutering can help to reduce the overall testosterone levels to make intros easier, but it's probably not something you'd want to do routinely.

Adult doe to adult doe

This is more likely to succeed than adult buck intros, but again it's really down to the temperament of the rats.

Putting their cages next to each other first

This can be a useful way to let two groups get to know one another, or to let adults get used to the smell of babies. It does help to allow new rats to 'settle' into your routine and spend some time on the same diet at your previous rats.

Bare cage intros

I use this method a lot. You take a fairly small cage that neither group is used to, add substrate, food and water, and put all the rats in together. If you're worried about how it will go, have the cage in a rat safe area with the top unclipped. Have a water spray bottle handy to surprise them into stopping if a fight does break out, and a cushion to separate rats if it really goes badly.

Keep them together in this small cage until they are sleeping in one heap. This might happen almost immediately, or it may take a day or two. Although they will make you feel very guilty for confining them in a tiny cage with strangers, the stress of being in a small space will help them to start to accept one another.

Once they're getting along well, you can move them into a bigger bare cage – either the one they'll be living in eventually, or if that's really large then an intermediate sized cage. If the cage belongs to either group, clean it out thoroughly. You can then start to add hammocks, ropes and hidey holes to the cage, but if they start to fight over these then take things back a step until they calm down again.

Once you've done a few intros you will begin to know when you can speed up this process and when you need to take it slowly. Don't worry, if it goes wrong you can always back up again.

Neutral territory intros

This is another popular way of introducing new rats. Find a neutral, rat safe place and allow the rats to meet one another for five minutes at a time, for a couple of times a day. Gradually extend this time until you're happy that they're getting along. Once they seem to have accepted one another, they can move into a cage together. It helps if the cage is either new to both groups, or has been cleaned out and rearranged. Don't add any defendable hidey holes until you're sure they're integrated.

18

FEEDING

Rats are omnivores just like ourselves, and are such food oriented animals that it seems unfair to provide a bland, homogenous diet such as pellets or nuggets. My approach is to try to feed a varied and healthy diet and assume that they'll pick up the nutrients they need from that.

A good rat muesli, or a muesli type rabbit mix, plus a little additional protein in the form of a small amount of dry dog food or leftover bones, should give them a good base diet. This can be supplemented with fruit and vegetables, a little fish oil, and calcium supplements, plus vitamin boosts such as Dr Squiggles Daily Essentials (although if they're not used to greens then it's best to increase the quantities gradually). If you're really keen, there's a book called 'The Scuttling Gourmet' by Alison Campbell, which is full of ideas for feeding your rats. A useful website is www.ratrations.com, which takes some of the guesswork out of providing a balanced diet.

Suitable vegetables are basically anything that a human can eat, with green veg such as curly kale and pak choi being especially good. Most fruits are appreciated, although those with stones should have the stone removed, and citrus should be avoided for male rats. If feeding banana, mind your fingers! Although rats enjoy just about any food, they won't miss unhealthy treats if you don't lead them to expect it. They don't need crisps, pizza and chocolate!

One way to provide added enrichment for your rats is to scatter their dry food in their cage substrate so that they have to forage for it. This also helps to prevent the greediest rats from grabbing all of the best bits. It's no less hygienic than bowl feeding, given that rats commonly take their food into the litter tray to eat anyway.

Keeping your rats' weight at a sensible level is one of the best ways to keep them healthy, so if they're starting to become a little overweight cut back on the food and try to encourage more exercise.

Nuts

Nuts in their shells are a wonderful combination of treat and toy. They're not something to be given too often due to their fat content, but will give your rats a challenge. Hazelnuts will last a minute or two, walnuts a little longer, and a brazil nut can take a sustained effort to break into.

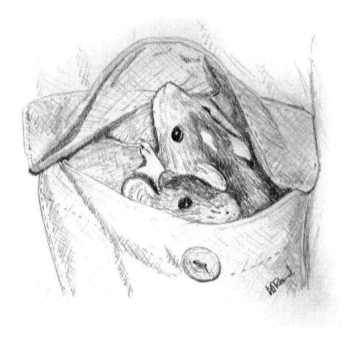

PLAYTIME

Confident handling

You can't expect your rats to be confident with you unless you're confident with them. You need to be able to scoop them up with a firm and confident grip, but not holding too tight. Don't try to restrain them or lift them by their tails, as you risk giving a painful injury to the tail, especially to an adult rat. Once you have them, let them climb on you. Most rats are very capable of holding onto you, and may come to enjoy riding on your shoulder as you walk around.

Where to play

Your rats will enjoy being allowed out of their cage each day to interact with you and explore their environment. The area needs to be made safe, with no cables to chew and places to injure themselves. They also have a taste for remote/phone buttons.

On the table

A table can be a handy place to let your rats play without giving them the run of a room. Rats are much more sensible about not jumping down than some other small rodents. Cover the table with a waterproof sheet or cut some old cushion flooring to size, and then add toys and rats.

In the hallway

If your household isn't constantly in and out of the hallway, this can give you a room without wires and tempting hidey holes.

In the bathroom

Again, the bathroom gives you a place without wires and usually with an easily wipeable floor. Make sure there are no holes next to pipes that they can disappear into, and remember to keep the toilet lid down.

In the living room

You can just put up with the mess they make and let them loose in your living room. Move any wires out of the way or use trunking to protect them and make sure there are no holes in the base of your furniture they can disappear into. Beware of holes in your sofa – if there are none to start with, they may appear spontaneously.

In their own rat room

This is the ideal, if you have the space. Giving the rats their own room means you can just open the cage and let them out to play. From experience they are still safer with supervision, but if there is space to set your toys out too it can become your own refuge as well.

In a playpen

An alternative to the table is to build a playpen for the rats – basically a wall to keep them in. Keep in mind that they can jump very well, so the height needs to be at least 75cm. If you want to be able to get in there with them, which is the ideal, then it also needs to be short enough for you to step over. Cardboard won't hold ratties for long, so the simplest way is to use hardboard or corrugated plastic, hinged with strong tape, and with an overlap that you can wedge or clip together.

Games to play

Pounce and tickle

Some rats just love playing games with your hand, so you can creep up behind them, pounce on them, tickle them and generally behave like a fellow rat. Be careful this doesn't wind them up to the point where they go and begin a fight with a cagemate.

Pea fishing

Pea fishing is an excellent game for cooling rats in hot weather. There are so many ways to set this up that I can't describe them all, but my preference is to use a reasonably deep but small storage box on top of plastic sheeting and an old towel to protect the floor. Add a rock or upturned bowl for the rats to stand on, put some pebbles and shells in the bottom and fill with water, then add frozen peas. Some rats will take to the game instantly, others will be hesitant. Some will sit on the rock and fish with their paws, others will snorkel around the bottom, eyes open, looking for the peas. But every single one will peel the peas and leave the shells.

Feather toys

For some reason, rats are fascinated by feathers (a good reason to keep them away from any pet birds). Cat chase toys with feathers are a fantastic way to interact with your rats, although as usual some rats will enjoy this more than others. You never know, it may be your lazy boys who surprise you with their enthusiasm for the game.

TRAINING

Using a litter tray

I like my rats to use a litter tray because it keeps the rest of the cage much fresher, and because they will then learn to use a tray when out and about in the room. Some owners find it useful to use a different substrate for the litter trays, but I've had success using the same substrate for the whole cage.

Put the litter tray(s) at the back of the cage, in the darkest corners, as these are the places the rats will tend to use even without a tray. If you find any poo outside the tray, move it into the tray. It can help to give the tray a quick spray of a strong smelling substance such as perfume, as this seems to spur the rats on to try and cover the smell with their own. Once you have trained your first group of rats, any others added to the group seem to be trained by the incumbent rats.

If you're hoping to use a tray during freerange, again put it in the darkest corner of the room and follow the same process.

Coming when called

Rats can be trained to recognise their own name and to come when called. The easiest way to gain a rat's attention is with food, as most rats are very food oriented. Use something small such as a tiny piece of bread, or even a piece of food from their own ration, and say their name whenever you give them a piece. It won't take long before they get the idea.

I recall my groups from freerange by feeding them their mix as soon as they come back. I use a small handbell to call them, and it's very amusing to watch them file back up the ramp into the cage. Shaking a food pot or crumpling a plastic carrier bag are other noises that carry well for the rats and get their attention well.

Performing tricks

Rats are very capable of learning to do tricks, and although I haven't attempted this with my own I've seen some very impressive videos online. They can also be clicker trained.

SHOWING

Rat shows are a fantastic way to meet other ratty people, to find interesting rat goodies to buy, and to show everyone how wonderful your rats are. Check the rules first to make sure you can take rats along as 'shoulder rats' (taken as companions rather than to show), but if you can, that is a wonderful way to meet people as they will come up and talk to your rats and break the ice that way. Before you consider taking your rats to a show, they need to be healthy and without any infection or parasites, and to have had no contact with other rats of unknown health during the past two weeks. It's very easy for infection to spread at a show, especially among shoulder rats, and although it helps to build the communal immunity it's a good idea to keep the risks as low as possible.

Most clubs have a 'how to show' section on their website so you can see how their shows work. The UK clubs tend to have two sections, pets and varieties. Both of these sections are judged on their health and condition, with the pet section also being judged on the rats' pet qualities such as tractability and outright lovability, and the varieties being judged on their conformity to the published standards for their variety. I'd recommend entering the pets section first while you learn the ropes, and moving on to varieties as you gain experience.

The prizes at most shows are rosettes, although some shows will have cups to win too. Don't hang the rosettes on your rat carrier unless you want them redesigned.

BREEDING

It is an extremely good idea to keep rats purely as pets for at least couple of years before you venture into breeding, to give you an idea of the time and money investment they require.

I would also recommend joining a regional club such as The Midlands Rat Club, the UK's national club (The National Fancy Rat Society), or both, attending rat shows and becoming active on club forums so that your name and your face become known and you have a ready source of advice and support. Get to know the people, the varieties of rats, and what your aim is in breeding.

Your aims

Your first task is to work out what you are trying to achieve by breeding. Do you want to create perfect pet rats? Do you want to make a particular colour or marking and win shows? Do you want to make very healthy and long lived rats? Or are you like most of us and you'd like to do all of these things at once?

Finding your foundation rats

Now you need to find the perfect rats to begin your line with. If your hope is to breed from a rat you already own, you need to consider its history. If your rats are from a breeder, talk to the breeder and ask for details of the parents and litter-mates, how their health and temperament has been, and ask for permission to breed on from the rats. If your rats are from a rescue or a petshop, it's inadvisable to use them to begin a line as you don't know what problems they may carry. Many rescue centres will have asked you to sign a no breeding contract at the point of homing.

If you don't already own the rats you need to achieve your breeding aims, now is the time to begin networking within the rat fancy. Find out who breeds rats with the pet qualities you most value, the variety you would like to breed, or who is breeding towards the same lifespan goals. Ask them to keep you in mind for kittens when they have their next litters. Bring in males first, then females, and more of each than you think you will need so that you have a choice when the time comes to mate up. These rats are the beginning of something great, so they have to be the right ones.

Choosing a rattery name

Naming your rattery is a useful way to identify your rats. In the UK ratteries use a prefix, a name that comes before the individual rat name, to identify which breeder the rat was bred by. Try to pick a name that means something to you and will stay relevant in coming years. It's also a good idea to do a web search to see if any other ratteries are using the name, to save confusion in the future.

There is no obligation to register your rattery name in the UK, and many perfectly valid and ethical breeders are not registered in this way. Having said this, the National Fancy Rat Society keeps a register of rattery names which is useful to allow you to see what names are already in use and to let you reserve a name for your own rattery. You will need to be a member for one year before you can register a name. Registering your rattery also allows you to begin working towards a 'stud name', achieved by winning at shows.

Mating age

Opinions on the ideal age to mate your does are incredibly varied. Some lines are better mated sooner because the does put weight on early and become less fertile. Some lines are better mated up later because the does are slow to mature. Ask the breeder who bred your does what age they are best bred from.

I generally mate up my does at between six months and a year old, usually closer to a year. This is because I like to give them time to play and enjoy their lives before they have the stress of bringing up babies, and because it allows me to exclude any that have health problems before this age. There is also a theory that does that are fertile to an older age are likely to live longer and pass on the trait, so I prefer to leave them longer and take the disappointment if they will not breed.

Bucks are better left a little longer, usually past one year old, to allow any hormonal aggression to show up. This can be hereditary so I would avoid breeding from an aggressive buck.

Mating up

Female rats generally come into season once every four or five days, and once mated the gestation period is 21 to 24 days, most commonly 22.5 days but varying between lines. The day of mating is day 0.

Many breeders mate up two pairs at once, to provide a backup in case of problems. Rat mothers are very maternal and invariably willing to foster babies. An alternative is to coordinate your litter with another breeder who lives nearby.

There are two common ways of pairing rats for breeding. The first is to wait until the doe is in season, and then place her in a small cage with the buck overnight. If your doe isn't having obvious seasons, you can test the pair each evening. It will be obvious when she is ready for mating as she will freeze in position waiting for the male. If she's karate kicking him instead, she's not ready yet.

The second way of pairing rats is to simply house the doe and buck together and wait until she begins to look pregnant, then remove the buck. I don't use this method as it can be difficult to reintroduce the buck to his cage-group afterwards.

Birth

A few days before their due date, many does become unsettled and more aggressive than usual with their cage-mates. If this happens, you need to make the decision whether or not to move her to a birthing cage now or wait a few days. If she seems fine, then wait until day 20 or 21 to move her into a smaller cage with narrow spaced bars to await her litter. Most does take birthing in their stride and it's better to just leave her to it, as checking too much can make you both nervous. Mum will birth each baby separately, eat the placenta and cord and then clean the baby thoroughly before tucking it underneath her.

Potential problems

Phantom pregnancy – a doe mated to an infertile buck may show all the signs of being pregnant, only to start shrinking again after day 17 or so.

Reabsorption – rats are able to 'change their minds' about being pregnant and may reabsorb the litter right up to the last minute. If this happens, keep an eye on your doe as there may be babies that are not fully absorbed and in this case she may develop an infection that requires antibiotic treatment.

Late birth – if the litter goes past its due date there is still hope, but keep a very close eye out for infection. Rats can delay the litter for up to ten days or so if they are very stressed, but this is very unusual in a well-nourished doe with a planned litter.

Stillbirth – it is not unusual for individuals or even a whole litter to be stillborn. You may not even see the babies, as mum's instinct is to 'clean up' and eat the bodies.

Stuck babies – if a baby gets stuck in the birth canal it can be very tiring for the mum, and she is not likely to be able to feed any of the babies she already has. You will need to consult your vet, and may have to have your doe spayed. If you have a foster mum handy, any babies already born should be fostered over, and any babies removed by caesarean may possibly survive to be fostered.

Lack of milk – newborn rats have very transparent skin and it is possible to see the milk in their stomachs if mum will let you. If they have not been fed, there is a chance the doe will settle to feed them, she may need moving to a carrier or small cage to encourage her, or they may be better fostered. This is a difficult decision and one that needs to be made on a case by case basis.

Dying in the nest – babies quite often 'disappear' from the nest, even up to a couple of weeks old. Usually this is because they have died and mum has 'cleaned up'. It's normal and something you just have to be prepared for.

Scattered babies – some mums are very upset by the birth and scatter their babies instead of caring for them. Move her and her babies into a small carrier or hamster cage until the nurturing instinct kicks in.

Handling

Baby rats can be handled from a day or two old, although it's best to move mum out of sight first. I usually tempt her out with some scrambled egg or similar yummy food to let me quickly check the babies on the first day. Later on, I put her back with her cage-group a couple of times a day and handle the babies for a few minutes. Handling them will prompt mum to groom them more, which strengthens her bond with them and also makes them calmer and less nervous as adults.

LIFE STAGES

Rats are very undeveloped when they are born, being completely naked, blind and dependent on their mother, who needs to be fed a high nutrient diet while nursing them. At around two weeks their eyes open, and they start to leave the nest and explore the cage soon after this. They will begin to try solid food by three weeks old, and enjoy high protein/carb weaning mixes, but are still taking a lot of nutrition from their mother. Males should be removed from their mother and sisters before five weeks old, at which age babies have been known to become fertile. The females can stay with mum for now. Both sexes benefit very much from another couple of weeks of familiar care before homing, so are usually homed at six or seven weeks, or even later if they are small for their age.

Rats are classed as 'kittens' up until 13 weeks of age, although they continue growing until 6 to 8 months old and bucks sometimes muscle up more after this. Bucks often stop taking as much exercise after this age, and with both sexes you need to be careful not to let them become overweight, as this will shorten their lives.

There is a large variation from rat to rat as to when they begin to look old. The average age for rats in the UK is around two years, but it's not uncommon to lose an 18 month old and, of course, many rats reach 2 ½ years or more. The belief that dumbo eared rats live longer than top eared rats is a myth, the only difference being the lower ear position as shown on the illustrations above. Older rats become more prone to respiratory problems, mammary tumours and hind leg degeneration, and can benefit from a diet with slightly lower levels of protein to reduce the load on their kidneys.

GENERAL CARE

Cage cleaning

If you litter train your rats, it makes it easy to do a quick exchange of the litter tray every day or two. It's a good idea to set a regular schedule for fully cleaning out your rat cage. How often you will need to clean out depends on the number of rats you have, how large the cage base is and what litter you use, but I would say a fortnight is the longest you would want to leave the cage.

Change out any hammocks that have been peed on, take the wheel out (if you have one) and any toys to rinse, empty out the litter and wipe out the base. Then spend some happy time rearranging the cage. I like to let the rats 'help' while I'm doing this, but if you'd rather not have their help you can pop them into their carrier or a small cage while you clean their cage.

Avoid using strong smelling cleansers, as these will prompt the rats to attempt to cover the smell with their own.

Water

Water is usually best in a pet water bottle attached to the cage rather than in a bowl, although bowls are sometimes better for older rats who can't sit up to drink. Water bottles should be refilled regularly, at least every second day, even if they haven't been emptied. I prefer to hang two bottles on each cage in case the spout fails on one of them. I use my usual fluoridated tap water for my rats, and don't believe it's caused them any problems over the years.

Nail clipping

Rats have sharp little nails. On the one hand it's useful, because it means they can climb up you and hang on well. On the other, it means they will leave scratches all over any bare skin. There are various ideas that come up now and again, such as using rocks or bricks under the water bottle or using perches and shelves made from rough materials to wear their nails down. My experience is that unless you have one of the wonderful rats who actually trims their own nails, you will need to trim them on occasion. If you're going to enter your rats in a show, they will need their nails trimming. At many shows you can prearrange for someone to show you how to do this, but the essence of it is as follows:

You will need either a pair of animal nail scissors, which have a notch in the blade for the nail to sit into, or a pair of nail clippers for people. My preference is for the nail clippers, but it's an individual thing. It's also useful to have some blood-stop powder or a small amount of cornflour on hand in case the nail gets cut a little too short. Get someone to help you. It is possible to do this alone, but I would save the attempt until your rat is more used to having his or her nails clipped. The holder needs to hold the rat belly outwards but against their chest, with the paws sticking outwards. Hold the rat's foot and look for the white area at the end. With most rats you can see through the nail to where the blood supply stops and where it's safe to clip. If the nail is curled round very close to the toe, put your own nail down the gap to shield it as you cut. Clip squarely across the tip of the nail, and move along as quickly as you can. Take care, because the rats will push their feet as well as pulling, and may well get their whiskers in the way if you do their front paws as well.

Bathing your rats

Rats very rarely need to be bathed; it's usually the cage that smells rather than the rat. If there's a smell that you can't clear by cleaning the cage and changing the hammocks, check the bars and the wall behind the cage before you start rat bathing.

If you feel you must bathe your rat, use a baby shampoo or pet shampoo. Fill the sink before you bring the rat into the room, and have a towel to hand in advance. If possible, sit down with the towel on your lap and then lower your rat into the water. Retrieve the rat from the top of your head, and work in a very small amount of shampoo. Rinse your rat in the water, retrieve them from behind your neck, and wrap them in the towel to dry and comfort them.

You will now need to grovel and offer treats to your rat before they will deign to notice you again.

HEALTH CARE

Rats are not as healthy as some other small mammals. If you are not prepared to spend money on vet care, please don't choose rats as your pet.

This is a fairly brief overview of some of the common illnesses. Although I've seen most of these problems, I'm not an expert and am usually guided by my vets.

It's not something you always think of when you choose rats as your pets, but it's as well to know where your vet is and what level of experience they have with rats before you need to visit in a hurry.

First Aid Box
The following items are useful first aid items for your rat. This could be expanded greatly, but these are the basics.

- Blood-stop powder – useful for pulled nails and bitten ears.

- Cotton wool balls – for cleaning wounds

- Hibiscrub – disinfectant for cleaning wounds

- Wound gel for abscess holes and wounds

- Small syringes for giving meds or flushing abscesses

- Ivermectin spot on for parasite infestations

- Microwave heat pad

Nursing Care
Ill rats are generally less stressed when left with their cage-mates, but there are occasions when they need to be removed to a hospital cage, either alone or with a gentle companion. If they feel cold to the touch, use a heat pad under one side of the hospital cage, but be sure to leave them the option of moving off the heat. If your rat is not grooming itself then you may need to wipe it down with a damp cloth, and wipe any urine away so it does not burn. Some rats seem to prefer to be with you

when they are ill, so if this seems to be the case try to find a way to keep them comfortable with you, but don't forget to offer water.

Medicating

I'm generally in favour of persuasion rather than force, but there are occasions when it just doesn't work. Liquid meds and pills that can be crushed can quite often be hidden in cream cheese, chocolate spread or other strong flavoured spreads, or my favourite method is to use a cube of bread and either drop liquid meds into it, or put a small amount of butter on top and pick up the powdered pill with it.

Liquid meds can also be syringed (with a needle-less syringe) into the corner of your rat's mouth, if necessary while the rat is wrapped in a towel and held by someone else.

Quarantining and infection control

Bringing new rats into your home will always pose a risk to your current rats, but there are ways that you can reduce the risk. If you're bringing rats in from a friend who you know well and trust, and whose rats are known to be healthy, then the risk is low. If you have picked up pet shop or rescue rats from poor conditions then the risk is higher. In general, new rats should be quarantined for at least two weeks, preferably in a separate airspace, and always seeing to the new rats second. You may also wish to treat the new rats for parasites as a preventative measure. In practice, many of us don't have the space for strict quarantine and have to compromise.

Parasites

Mites

Mites often appear with no apparent origin, but the assumption is that they find their way in via the substrate or food. Signs of mites include increased scratching, scabs and scratches around the neck, and sometimes flaky skin. You cannot see them with the naked eye. It often looks as though rats have been fighting when in reality they have mite infestations, so it's always worth treating for mites if your rats have bites but you haven't seen them fighting.

Lice

You may see the 'nits' or eggs as white specks in the fur, or just notice the lice as brown or orange specks marching along parted hairs.

Sarcoptic Mange mites

These mites create bobbles and growths on the rats' ears and nose, spreading to the feet, tail and genitals. They are very infectious between rats.

Parasite treatment

The treatment I would recommend for all of the above parasites is Ivermectin, either in a 'spot on' form or injected by your vet. Bear in mind that this is a poison and can cause neurological damage if overdosed, so weigh your rat first and stick to the instructions on the packet.

For ordinary mites you generally only need to treat the affected rats. For lice and mange mites, I would recommend treating all of your rats.

Infections

Abscesses

Rats are unfortunately very good at producing abscesses. I'd advise an inexperienced rat owner to visit the vet with these, as they usually need draining before they will heal. If the vet decides to open up the abscess, it's useful to ask them to make a hole rather than a slit so that it won't heal up too quickly. A course of antibiotics can help to clear the infection, and flushing the abscess through with sterile water or an antibacterial will also help.

Mycoplasma

This is the one that everyone blames for respiratory disease, and is endemic in the pet rat population. It tends to be a slow progressive disease which lays the way for other secondary infections of the lungs. It can also be a cause of pyometra.

CK, or Corynebacterium Kutscheri

This is a nasty bacteria which can cause a very quick death when it infects the lungs. The symptoms are silent laboured breathing and weight loss, often after a trigger event such as an operation or treatment with steroids. It causes progressive lung abscesses and is often only diagnosed if a post mortem is done. If the rat does survive then it is left with permanent lung damage. This bacteria can also infect other organs, again producing numerous abscesses.

SDAV

Sialodacryoadenitis or Rat Coronavirus is generally at a fairly low level in the pet rat population, but every now and then it flares up and gets passed around via pet suppliers and rat shows. Symptoms can include swollen eyes, respiratory distress and weight loss, sometimes leading to death.

Sendai

This is another disease often passed on via pet suppliers and rat shows and produces flu-like symptoms and dehydration, sometimes leading to death. Antibiotics can be useful against secondary infections.

Pyometra

Does can suffer from pus or blood in the uterus, showing as bleeding or as a swollen abdomen. Antibiotics can sometimes clear up bleeding, but spaying is the only sure treatment.

Other conditions

Porphyrin staining

Rats' tears contain a red stain called porphyrin, which acts as a useful sign when they are having eye problems or upper respiratory infections. If this persists then a visit to the vet is in order.

Diabetes

This is due to a problem with insulin production, with the symptoms being increased drinking, and weight loss. The rat should have access to water at all times and be fed a diet with as little sugar and refined carbohydrate as possible. It is possible to use injected insulin to treat this, under a vet's advice.

Head tilt

The symptoms, fairly obviously, are the head tilted to one side and 'rolling' or circling when trying to walk. This is usually an inner ear infection and generally responds to steroids and antibiotics, although the sooner it's treated the more chance of the tilt going away. Often the underlying infection is cured but the tilt remains, although it sometimes improves over time.

Mammary lumps

These are generally just fatty lumps under the legs or on the lower neck. They don't tend to be cancerous and can be removed fairly routinely if they're not left to become enormous and are not too close to the genitals. In my experience they don't always come back if removed and if the rat is otherwise fit and healthy I see no reason why they shouldn't be removed.

Tumours

There are, of course, other tumours that are found to be cancerous. Again, if the rat is fit and healthy and the vet feels there is a good chance of removing the tumour, I would go for removal. If the tumour looks cancerous or returns quickly, then it's time to think again. Some owners have had success using Tamoxifen to treat tumours, although this doesn't always work and the side effects can lead to rats refusing to take it.

Pituitary or brain tumours

These cause neurological problems such as progressive loss of grip with the hands, and can be detected at an early stage by touching the rat's head and seeing if they 'head bump', pushing up against the pressure.

Zymbal's gland tumours

The Zymbal's gland sits at the base of the ear canal. The tumour often shows up as a fairly ordinary abscess just below and behind the ear, or sometimes as a pus discharge from the ear. The abscess doesn't clear, and if operated on then a tumour is found beneath that is producing the infected material, and is impossible to remove entirely.

Hind leg degeneration

Hind leg degeneration is usually a disease of older rats, usually coming on slowly with just a slight weakness and knuckling under of the back feet at first, progressing to paralysis of the legs. When it comes on quickly I would suspect an injury or a brain problem. There are various ideas for treatment, none of which seems to work on all cases. NSAIDs can help some rats, but can hasten kidney disease in others.

Tooth problems

Rats' teeth are normally orange, so this is nothing to worry about. The most common problems are broken or overgrowing teeth. If your rat breaks a tooth, you may have to have the opposing teeth trimmed until the broken tooth regrows. Sometimes teeth become misaligned as rats grow older and may have to have regular trims every two or three weeks.

Zoonoses

(Diseases that you and your other pets can share with your rats)

Ringworm

This is a fungal infection that can give your rats a circular patch of bare skin, and on you produces a circular inflammation on the skin that spreads outwards like a toadstool ring. It's passed easily from person to person and from person to rat and back again, so you can never be really sure who brought it home, but you're the one who's been out in the infectious world.

Staphylococcus aureus

Cuts or scratches on both humans and rats can pick up staph infections, and you can pass them to each other, so be aware that this is what a skin infection may be.

Bordatella

Rats have been known to pick up Bordatella from live vaccine used on dogs, so it's a good idea to keep your rats quarantined from your dogs when they've had their kennel cough vaccination.

Hantavirus

Some pet rats in the UK have been found to carry Hantavirus. This doesn't seem to cause the rats any problems, but in rare cases can cause fever, headaches and renal problems in humans. It seems to usually be a mild infection but can cause serious illness and is probably passed on by inhaling dust while cleaning cages.

Toxoplasmosis

You're not likely to know whether or not your rats have this, but again it's something that you're more likely to catch from a pet that goes outdoors than from a caged pet rat. In humans this is a mild infection that is only really a problem if you're pregnant. The usual advice is to avoid handling pet faeces while pregnant, so I would recommend using it as a good excuse to get someone else to clean cages for you.

Weil's disease (Leptospirosis)

I've included this because it's something that people think of in connection with wild rats. It is not commonly found in pet rats.

This is a bacterial disease which crosses the species barrier to affect many animals, including rats and humans and also cattle, dogs, horses and pigs. Pet rats have very little opportunity to contract this disease, and you are probably more likely to catch it from a pet dog that has been swimming in the local river than from your pet rat.

The symptoms in humans are a 'flu-like' illness which can last from a few days to a few weeks, and which like flu is very occasionally fatal. There are around 2 or 3 human deaths from Leptospirosis each year in the UK, and it is mostly a danger to farmers and cavers who can come into contact with the urine of infected animals.

FURTHER READING

Books

I love rats, I do! – by Annette Rand

The Happy Rat Handbook – by Annette Rand

The Rat's Whiskers – by Annette Rand

The NFRS Handbook Part One - Common Diseases of the Fancy Rat – by Ann Storey

The Scuttling Gourmet – A guide to wholesome nutrition for rats – by Alison Campbell

Websites

http://www.rattycorner.com/

http://ratguide.com/

http://www.rathealth.co.uk/

http://www.fancyratsforum.co.uk/

http://www.ratrations.com/

http://www.bettysbeds.com/

http://www.fuzzbutt.co.uk/

http://www.littlepetwarehouse.co.uk/

http://www.ratwarehouse.com/

UK Rat Clubs

There are rat clubs, and then there are rat clubs. Check out the websites to see which one appeals to you – you don't have to join the nearest one! I'd recommend the Midlands Rat Club, but then I'm on the committee so I may be a little biased.

The Midlands Rat Club - http://www.midlandsratclub.org/

The North of England Rat Society - http://www.neratsociety.co.uk/

The Scottish Rat Club - http://www.scottishratclub.co.uk/

The Yorkshire Rat Club - http://yorkshireratclub.org.uk/

The London and Southern Counties Rat and Mouse Club - http://www.miceandrats.com/

The National Fancy Rat Club - http://www.nfrs.org/

ABOUT THE AUTHOR

Annette Rand is a breeder of pet rats in the UK, breeding under the name of Brandywine Stud. She is a member of the National Fancy Rat Society, Midlands Rat Club and North of England Rat Society, and maintains the rattycorner.com website with details of her adventures in rat keeping.

Printed in Great Britain
by Amazon